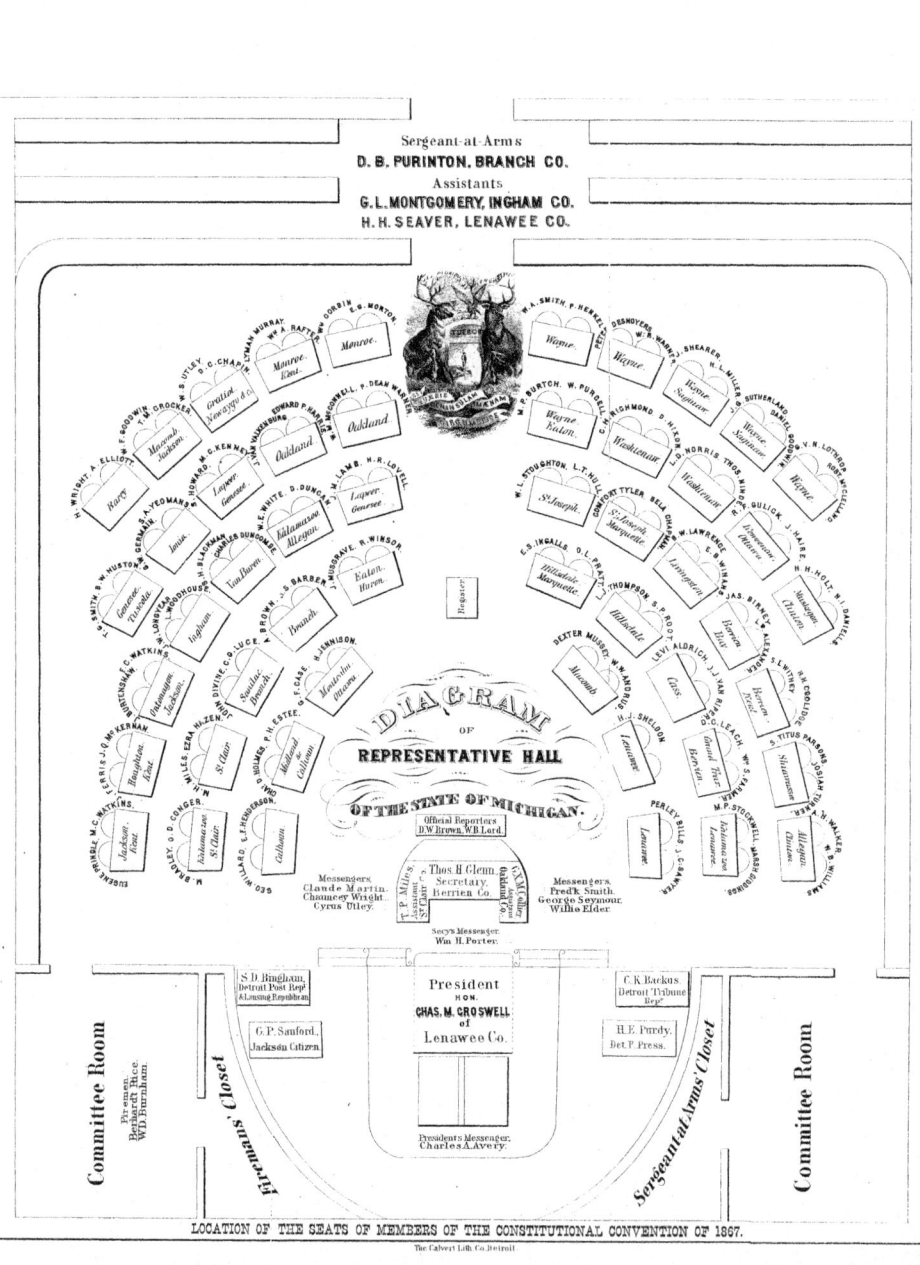

MANUAL

OF THE

Constitutional Convention,

OF THE

STATE OF MICHIGAN.

BEGUN IN THE CAPITOL, AT LANSING,

MAY 15, A. D. 1867.

BY AUTHORITY.

LANSING, MICHIGAN:
JOHN A. KERR & CO., PRINTERS TO THE STATE.
1867.

CALENDAR, 1867.

1867.	Sunday.	Monday.	Tuesday.	Wednesday.	Thursday.	Friday.	Saturday.	1867.	Sunday.	Monday.	Tuesday.	Wednesday.	Thursday.	Friday.	Saturday.
JAN.	..	..	1	2	3	4	5	JULY.	..	1	2	3	4	5	6
	6	7	8	9	10	11	12		7	8	9	10	11	12	13
	13	14	15	16	17	18	19		14	15	16	17	18	19	20
	20	21	22	23	24	25	26		21	22	23	24	25	26	27
	27	28	29	30	31	..	..		28	29	30	31	..	..	..
FEB.	..	..	..	..	..	1	2	AUG.	..	..	..	..	1	2	3
	3	4	5	6	7	8	9		4	5	6	7	8	9	10
	10	11	12	13	14	15	16		11	12	13	14	15	16	17
	17	18	19	20	21	22	23		18	19	20	21	22	23	24
	24	25	26	27	28	..	..		25	26	27	28	29	30	31
MAR.	..	..	..	..	..	1	2	SEPT.	1	2	3	4	5	6	7
	3	4	5	6	7	8	9		8	9	10	11	12	13	14
	10	11	12	13	14	15	16		15	16	17	18	19	20	21
	17	18	19	20	21	22	23		22	23	24	25	26	27	28
	24	25	26	27	28	29	30		29	30	..	..	..	..	..
	31	..	..	..	..	..	..								
APRIL.	..	1	2	3	4	5	6	OCT.	..	..	1	2	3	4	5
	7	8	9	10	11	12	13		6	7	8	9	10	11	12
	14	15	16	17	18	19	20		13	14	15	16	17	18	19
	21	22	23	24	25	26	27		20	21	22	23	24	25	26
	28	29	30	..	..	..	..		27	28	29	30	31	..	..
MAY.	..	..	..	1	2	3	4	NOV.	..	..	..	..	..	1	2
	5	6	7	8	9	10	11		3	4	5	6	7	8	9
	12	13	14	15	16	17	18		10	11	12	13	14	15	16
	19	20	21	22	23	24	25		17	18	19	20	21	22	23
	26	27	28	29	30	31	..		24	25	26	27	28	29	30
JUNE.	..	..	..	..	..	..	1	DEC.	1	2	3	4	5	6	7
	2	3	4	5	6	7	8		8	9	10	11	12	13	14
	9	10	11	12	13	14	15		15	16	17	18	19	20	21
	16	17	18	19	20	21	22		22	23	24	25	26	27	28
	23	24	25	26	27	28	29		29	30	31	..	..	..	..
	30	..	..	..	..	..	..		..	..	..	..	..	..	..

CALENDAR, 1868.

1868.	Sunday.	Monday.	Tuesday.	Wednesday.	Thursday.	Friday.	Saturday.	1868.	Sunday.	Monday.	Tuesday.	Wednesday.	Thursday.	Friday.	Saturday.
Jan.	..	..	..	1	2	3	4	July.	..	..	..	1	2	3	4
	5	6	7	8	9	10	11		5	6	7	8	9	10	11
	12	13	14	15	16	17	18		12	13	14	15	16	17	18
	19	20	21	22	23	24	25		19	20	21	22	23	24	25
	26	27	28	29	30	31	..		26	27	28	29	30	31	..
Feb.	..	..	..	..	..	..	1	Aug.	..	..	..	..	..	..	1
	2	3	4	5	6	7	8		2	3	4	5	6	7	8
	9	10	11	12	13	14	15		9	10	11	12	13	14	15
	16	17	18	19	20	21	22		16	17	18	19	20	21	22
	23	24	25	26	27	28	29		23	24	25	26	27	28	29
Mar.	1	2	3	4	5	6	7		30	31	..	..	..	..	..
	8	9	10	11	12	13	14	Sept.	..	..	1	2	3	4	5
	15	16	17	18	19	20	21		6	7	8	9	10	11	12
	22	23	24	25	26	27	28		13	14	15	16	17	18	19
	29	30	31	..	..	..	..		20	21	22	23	24	25	26
April.	..	..	..	1	2	3	4		27	28	29	30	..	..	..
	5	6	7	8	9	10	11	Oct.	..	..	..	..	1	2	3
	12	13	14	15	16	17	18		4	5	6	7	8	9	10
	19	20	21	22	23	24	25		11	12	13	14	15	16	17
	26	27	28	29	30	..	..		18	19	20	21	22	23	24
May.	..	..	..	..	..	1	2		25	26	27	28	29	30	31
	3	4	5	6	7	8	9	Nov.	1	2	3	4	5	6	7
	10	11	12	13	14	15	16		8	9	10	11	12	13	14
	17	18	19	20	21	22	23		15	16	17	18	19	20	21
	24	25	26	27	28	29	30		22	23	24	25	26	27	28
	31	..	..	..	..	..	..		29	30	..	..	..	..	..
June.	..	1	2	3	4	5	6	Dec.	..	..	1	2	3	4	5
	7	8	9	10	11	12	13		6	7	8	9	10	11	12
	14	15	16	17	18	19	20		13	14	15	16	17	18	19
	21	22	23	24	25	26	27		20	21	22	23	24	25	26
	28	29	30	..	..	..	..		27	28	29	30	31	..	..

CALENDAR, 1869.

1869.	Sunday.	Monday.	Tuesday.	Wednesday.	Thursday.	Friday.	Saturday.	1869.	Sunday.	Monday.	Tuesday.	Wednesday.	Thursday.	Friday.	Saturday.
Jan.	..	..	..	..	..	1	2	July.	..	..	..	..	1	2	3
	3	4	5	6	7	8	9		4	5	6	7	8	9	10
	10	11	12	13	14	15	16		11	12	13	14	15	16	17
	17	18	19	20	21	22	23		18	19	20	21	22	23	24
	24	25	26	27	28	29	30		25	26	27	28	29	30	31
	31	..	..	..	..	..	..								
Feb.	..	1	2	3	4	5	6	Aug.	1	2	3	4	5	6	7
	7	8	9	10	11	12	13		8	9	10	11	12	13	14
	14	15	16	17	18	19	20		15	16	17	18	19	20	21
	21	22	23	24	25	26	27		22	23	24	25	26	27	28
	28	..	..	..	..	..	..		29	30	31	..	..	..	..
Mar.	..	1	2	3	4	5	6	Sept.	..	..	..	1	2	3	4
	7	8	9	10	11	12	13		5	6	7	8	9	10	11
	14	15	16	17	18	19	20		12	13	14	15	16	17	18
	21	22	23	24	25	26	27		19	20	21	22	23	24	25
	28	29	30	31	..	..	..		26	27	28	29	30	..	..
April.	..	..	..	..	1	2	3	Oct.	..	..	..	..	..	1	2
	4	5	6	7	8	9	10		3	4	5	6	7	8	9
	11	12	13	14	15	16	17		10	11	12	13	14	15	16
	18	19	20	21	22	23	24		17	18	19	20	21	22	23
	25	26	27	28	29	30	..		24	25	26	27	28	29	30
May.	..	..	..	..	..	..	1		31	..	..	..	..	..	..
	2	3	4	5	6	7	8	Nov.	..	1	2	3	4	5	6
	9	10	11	12	13	14	15		7	8	9	10	11	12	13
	16	17	18	19	20	21	22		14	15	16	17	18	19	20
	23	24	25	26	27	28	29		21	22	23	24	25	26	27
	30	31	..	..	..	..	..		28	29	30	..	..	..	..
June.	..	..	1	2	3	4	5	Dec.	..	..	..	1	2	3	4
	6	7	8	9	10	11	12		5	6	7	8	9	10	11
	13	14	15	16	17	18	19		12	13	14	15	16	17	18
	20	21	22	23	24	25	26		19	20	21	22	23	24	25
	27	28	29	30	..	..	..		26	27	28	29	30	31	..

CALENDAR, 1870.

1870.	Sunday.	Monday.	Tuesday.	Wednesday.	Thursday.	Friday.	Saturday.	1870.	Sunday.	Monday.	Tuesday.	Wednesday.	Thursday.	Friday.	Saturday.
Jan.	..	..	..	..	..	..	1	July.	..	..	..	..	..	1	2
	2	3	4	5	6	7	8		3	4	5	6	7	8	9
	9	10	11	12	13	14	15		10	11	12	13	14	15	16
	16	17	18	19	20	21	22		17	18	19	20	21	22	23
	23	24	25	26	27	28	29		24	25	26	27	28	29	30
	30	31	..	..	..	..	..		31	..	..	..	..	..	..
Feb.	..	..	1	2	3	4	5	Aug.	..	1	2	3	4	5	6
	6	7	8	9	10	11	12		7	8	9	10	11	12	13
	13	14	15	16	17	18	19		14	15	16	17	18	19	20
	20	21	22	23	24	25	26		21	22	23	24	25	26	27
	27	28	..	..	..	..	..		28	29	30	31	..	..	..
Mar.	..	..	1	2	3	4	5	Sept.	..	..	..	..	1	2	3
	6	7	8	9	10	11	12		4	5	6	7	8	9	10
	13	14	15	16	17	18	19		11	12	13	14	15	16	17
	20	21	22	23	24	25	26		18	19	20	21	22	23	24
	27	28	29	30	31	..	..		25	26	27	28	29	30	..
April.	..	..	..	..	..	1	2	Oct.	..	..	..	..	..	..	1
	3	4	5	6	7	8	9		2	3	4	5	6	7	8
	10	11	12	13	14	15	16		9	10	11	12	13	14	15
	17	18	19	20	21	22	23		16	17	18	19	20	21	22
	24	25	26	27	28	29	30		23	24	25	26	27	28	29
May.	1	2	3	4	5	6	7		30	31	..	..	..	..	..
	8	9	10	11	12	13	14	Nov.	..	..	1	2	3	4	5
	15	16	17	18	19	20	21		6	7	8	9	10	11	12
	22	23	24	25	26	27	28		13	14	15	16	17	18	19
	29	30	31	..	..	..	..		20	21	22	23	24	25	26
June.	..	..	..	1	2	3	4		27	28	29	30	..	..	..
	5	6	7	8	9	10	11	Dec.	..	..	..	..	1	2	3
	12	13	14	15	16	17	18		4	5	6	7	8	9	10
	19	20	21	22	23	24	25		11	12	13	14	15	16	17
	26	27	28	29	30	..	..		18	19	20	21	22	23	24
	..	..	..	..	..	..	..		25	26	27	28	29	30	31

IN CONVENTION, JUNE 13, 1867.

MANUAL OF THE CONVENTION.

Mr. VAN VALKENBURGH. I offer the following resolution:

Resolved, That the committee on printing be directed to procure the publishing of a Manual for the members of the Convention, containing the names of the delegates, the counties they represent, their post-office address, their occupations, and their respective boarding places in this city; also, a copy of the present Constitution, the rules of the Convention, and such other matter as they may deem expedient.

Mr. President, I offer this resolution from a belief that a Manual of the kind named would be of great value to members of this Convention, not only during their stay here, but when they shall have returned to their homes. I have in my hand, sir, a Manual prepared for the Convention of 1850, which embraces the information sought to be obtained by my resolution, and the autographs of the officers and members of that Convention, and also the autographs of the State officers. I have often found this Manual a great help to me in the past. We become acquainted with each other upon this floor; we may know what counties we respectively represent, but not knowing the particular locality, the post-office address, we cannot communicate with each other. This Manual obviates that difficulty.

Mr. President, I value this Manual highly for other reasons. I value it for the cherished memories it revives of the past—memories of noble men who stood shoulder to shoulder with me upon this floor, day after day, contending for the adoption of controverted principles in the Constitution, some of which were successfully urged, and I trust they will hold a place in all future Constitutions, as monuments of *their* fidelity and devotion to the right. Some of those men, though much my juniors, have long since paid the debt of nature, and preceded me to the eternal world. I hold, Mr. President, that this strangely maligned Constitution of ours, which has drawn forth so many maledictions from various sources, has still some redeeming features, some salient points, which will stand forth in all the future as oases to keep green the memory of their originators.

I also value this Manual, Mr. President, for its frequent revival of the dear memories of acquaintances made and friendships formed upon this floor with noble men, who battled valiantly in the cause of justice and humanity, and whose devotion to the right will always stand forth in bold relief, beckoning onward the timid and the fearful—who, although then defeated in some of their cherished purposes, still live to see those principles crowned triumphantly in this Convention, and to participate in their triumph, for I have the great pleasure of meeting some of those men once more upon this floor.

My good friend from Wayne, (Mr. SHEARER,) told us a day or two since of the rapid progress of this State; the many improvements made since his first advent to it; how the red man of the forest had faded away before the rapid advance of civilization; how the cultivated fields had taken the place of the dense forest, and the stately mansion supplanted the Indian wigwam. He told us of the appearance of this place at his first visit, how he came here in a lumbering stage coach, over roads almost impassable, and found only a site for a city. I, too, saw Lansing at an early day—in the autumn of 1847. Then a resident of Western New York, I was attracted to this place by the fame of your Capital, located in the wilderness. I also found my way here over roads unspeakably toilsome; and here, where Lansing now stands in all her beauty, I found a few small cottages erected in the forest upon imaginary streets, which had existence only upon paper; and here on this spot, Mr. President, where this Capitol now stands, I found sturdy men digging up the tall forest oaks to make way for the foundations of this structure. At that time—twenty years ago the coming autumn—Lansing was almost an unbroken wilderness. Now, how changed! As by the wand of magic, the forest has been converted into fruitful fields, and the wilderness made to bud and blossom like the rose. Compare for a moment, sir, the Lansing of 1847 with the Lansing of to-day—then a wilderness, the home of the wolf and the panther; now the gem of our State, the seat of civilization, of morality, of religion, of all that is fair and lovely and of good report, of all that renders life desirable, all that conduces to our happiness here and hereafter. Lansing, then a reproach to the legislators who located it here, is now the pride of our fair Peninsula.

Yes, sir, we may well be proud of our State Capital, with her broad, well-graded avenues, her extended sidewalks, her beautiful residences, her tasteful and highly ornamented gardens, her princely store-houses, her numerous places of religious worship, dotting her expanded area as landmarks to guide us to the better land, her talented and devoted clergy, her far-famed and well appointed Female College, an honor to any State, her other literary institutions, her public and private libraries, her courteous and hospitable citizens. Yes, sir, I repeat we may well be proud of the beautiful Capital of our beautiful Peninsula.

Who can tell the future of Lansing? Who can prophesy her *status* in twenty years to come, with her peerless location, her physical energies, her cultivated intellect, her moral eminence, her indomitable perseverance, in the midst of a peninsula unsurpassed for beauty and fertility in the wide world? Who can tell? Well may we exclaim, in the language of our State motto, "*Si quæris peninsulam amænam circumspice!*" Yes! if you wish to see a beautiful peninsula, look around—look to the east and west, to the north and south, and gaze upon as beautiful a scene as can be found under the broad canopy of the heavens. The gentleman from Wayne told us he loved the State of his adoption. Who marvels at it, sir? Who wonders that a man of his genial feelings, with his warm heart, should love this State of ours? I, too, sir, love the State of my adoption. The man who does not love her must be a stoic and an alien. I love her placid lakes, dotting her surface as the stars gem the firmament. I love her grand rivers and her purling streams; I love her majestic forests and her green fields; I love her brave men and her fair women; I encircle them in my arms, I press them to my heart. As I look around upon this Convention, its accomplished and efficient officers, its noble men, the bone and sinew of our State, the brain and intellect of our Peninsula, I am proud, sir, that I am a member of this body, proud that I have a standing upon this floor. It stirs the blood within me. As the field of battle arouses the energies of the old, worn war horse, so this arena stirs my blood and awakens the energies of former days. It makes me young again.

The Convention of 1850 contained some of the best men in our State—men who, like Saul, towered a head and shoulders above their coevals. It contained many good, devoted, patriotic men, whose memories are cherished, a blessing to our State and an honor to our common country. And still, Mr. President, no observing man can fail to see that the mental and moral progress of our State has kept pace fully with its physical advancement. But, Mr. President, I wander. I ask your pardon, sir—I ask pardon of the Convention. I return to the question. The adoption of the resolution can be of little avail to me—the time of my sojourn among you, in all human probability, will be brief. I have already passed the allotted age of man—three score and ten—and, in the language of the Psalmist, "if by reason of strength they reach four score years, yet is their strength labor and sorrow, for it is soon cut off and we fly away." My work here is nearly accomplished. I shall meet you no more for the revision of human laws; but I trust, I hope I may meet many of you—yea, all of you—in that Convention where the organic law is perfect, and no human passions or conflicting opinions mar its harmony.

Individually, I expect but little benefit from the adoption of this resolution; but assured, as I am, that it will be a great benefit to the young men, the business men, in this Convention, both in their social and business relations, I have been induced to offer the resolution, and I hope it will be adopted. The expense will be trifling compared with the benefit to be derived. Should it be adopted, I would suggest to the committee having charge of its publication some improvements upon the Manual of 1850—that is, to insert in some part of the Manual a few blank leaves of writing paper, upon which to obtain the autographs of the officers and members of the Convention. This was neglected in 1850, and we were obliged to use such blanks for that purpose as were incidentally left in the Manual.

Mr. WITHEY moved that the resolution and remarks of Mr. VAN VALKENBURGH be published in the Manual;

Which was unanimously adopted.

MEMBERS AND OFFICERS

OF THE

Constitutional Convention of the State of Michigan,

1867.

Hon. CHARLES M. CROSWELL, President, Lenawee County; Home Post Office, Adrian; Lodgings, Lansing House; Nativity, N. Y.; Profession, Lawyer; age, 41.

NAMES.	COUNTY.	HOME P. O.	LODGINGS.	NATIVITY.	PROFESSION.	AGE.
Aldrich, Levi,...	Cass,...	Edwardsburg,...	Lansing House,...	New York,...	Physician,...	47
Alexander, Lorenzo P....	Berrien,...	Buchanan,...	"	"	Merchant,...	46
Andrus, William W....	Macomb,...	Utica,...	"	"	Physician,...	46
Barber, Julius S....	Branch,...	Coldwater,...	"	Vermont,...	Merchant,...	43
Bills, Perley....	Lenawee,...	Tecumseh,...	"	"	Lawyer,...	56
Birney, James....	Bay,...	Bay City,...	"	Kentucky,...	"	49
Blackman, Samuel H....	Van Buren,...	Paw Paw,...	F. Davis,...	Ohio,...	"	53
Bradley, Milton....	Kalamazoo,...	Richland,...	Rev. Mr. Weed,...	New York,...	Clergyman,...	55
Brown, Asahel....	Branch,...	Algansee,...	Lansing House,...	N. J.,...	Farmer,...	64
Burtch, Milton P....	Eaton,...	Grand Ledge,...	H. Clippenger,...	New York,...	"	55
Burtenshaw, James....	Ontonagon,...	Ontonagon,...	Mrs. Lemley,...	England,...	Merchant,...	39
Case, George F....	Montcalm,...	Stanton,...	J. P. Baker,...	Vermont,...	Furniture Dealer,..	37
Chapin, De Witt C....	Gratiot,...	Alma,...	H. Clippenger,...	New York,...	Lawyer,...	50
Chapman, Bela....	Mackinac,...	Mackinac,...	Mrs. Bascom,...	N. H.,...	Merchant,...	74
Coolidge, Henry H....	Berrien,...	Niles,...	Lansing House,...	Mass.,...	Lawyer,...	55

MEMBERS OF CONVENTION. 19

Name	County	Post Office	Birthplace	Occupation	Age
Conger, Omar D.*	St. Clair,	Port Huron,	Lansing House,	New York,	Lawyer,	49
Corbin, William	Monroe,	Petersburg,	Dr. Wright,	"	Miscellaneous,	41
Crocker, Thomas M	Macomb,	Mt. Clemens,	Lansing House,	Vermont,	Lawyer,	41
Daniells, Nathaniel I.	Clinton,	Wacousta,	" "	New York,	Farmer,	59
Desnoyers, Peter	Wayne,	Detroit,	" "	Michigan,	"	67
Divine, John	Sanilac,	Lexington,	" "	Canada,	Lawyer,	43
Duncan, Delamore	Kalamazoo,	Schoolcraft,	S. R. Greene,	N. H.,	Farmer,	61
Duncombe, Charles	Van Buren,	Keeler,	F. Davis,	Canada,	"	45
Elliott, Adam	Barry,	Hickory Cor.	American,	England,	"	52
Estee, Perry H	Isabella,	Sa't River,	Lansing House,	New York,	Farmer,	42
Farmer, William S	Berrien,	Eau Claire,	Lansing House,	"	"	51
Ferris, Jacob	Kent,	Grand Rapids,	Mr. Paddack,	"	Lawyer,	45
Germain, George W	Ionia,	North Plains,	Mr. Ford,	"	Farmer,	49
Giddings, Marsh	Kalamazoo,	Kalamazoo,	Lansing House,	Conn.,	Lawyer,	50
Goodwin, William F*	Jackson,	Concord,	" "	New York,	Miller and Farmer,	54
Goodwin, Daniel	Wayne,	Detroit,	" "	"	Lawyer,	67
Gulick, R. bert F	Keweenaw,	Eagle River,	" "	"	"	36
Haire, John	Ottawa,	Grandville,	Lansing House,	Ireland,	Lumberman,	46
Harris, Edward P	Oakland,	Rochester,	American,	Mass.,	Lawyer,	64
Hazen, Ezra	St. Cair,	Memphis,	Lansing House,	New York,	Miscellaneous,	49
Henderson, Eden F	Calhoun,	Marshall,	" "	New York,	Farmer,	39
Henkel, Peter	Wayne,	Detroit,		Germany,	Merchant,	42
Hixson, Daniel	Washtenaw,	Clinton,	Edgar House,	New York,	Farmer,	64
Holmes, Charles D.	Calhoun,	Albion,	Mr. Brisbin,	Mass.,	"	52
Holt, Henry H	Muskegon,	Muskegon,	Lansing House,	New York,	Lawyer,	34
Howard, Sumner	Genesee,	Flint,	H. R. Pratt,	Mass.,	"	30
Hull, Levi T	St. Joseph,	Constantine,	Lansing House,		Printer,	39
Huston, Benjamin W	Tuscola,	Vassar,	Lansing House,	New York,	Lawyer,	36
Ingalls, Eleazer S	Menominee,	Menominee,	American,	N. H.,	Lawyer,	47
Jennison, Hiram	Ottawa,					
Kenny, Myron C	Lapeer,	Lapeer,	T. Ford,	N. Y.,	Physician,	44
Lamb, John M	"	Dryden,	Lansing House,	N. J.,	Various,	60
Lawrence, Benjamin W	Livingston,	Fowlerville,	G. Fowler,	Mass.,	Farmer,	55

MEMBERS OF CONVENTION.

LIST OF MEMBERS, &c.—Continued.

NAMES.	COUNTY.	HOME P. O.	LODGINGS.	NATIVITY.	PROFESSION.	AGE.
Leach Dewitt C	G'd Traverse	Traverse City,	Mrs. Northrop,	New York,	Farmer,	44
Longyear, John W	Ingham,	Lansing,	Home,	"	Lawyer,	46
Lothrop, Geo. V. N	Wayne,	Detroit,	Lansing House,	Mass.,	"	49
Lovell, Henry R	Genesee,	Flint,	H. R. Pratt,	Conn.,	"	35
Luce, Cyrus G	Branch,	Gilead,	Lansing House,	Ohio,	Farmer,	42
McClelland, Robert	Wayne,	Detroit,	"	Penn.,	Lawyer,	59
McConnell, Willard M	Oakland,	Pontiac,	"	New York,	Merchant,	53
McKernan, John Q	Houghton,	Houghton,		"	Carpenter & Millw't,	42
Miles, Marcus H	St. Clair,	St. Clair,	Lansing House,	"	Lawyer,	53
Miller, Hiram L	Saginaw,	Saginaw City,	Rev. Mr. Weed,	N. J.,	Farmer,	63
Morton, Edward G.*	Monroe,	Monroe,	Dr Wright's,	Vermont,	Printer,	50
Murray, Lyman	Kent,	Lisbon,	Dr. Bailey,	New York,	Farmer,	48
Mussey, Dexter	Macomb,	Romeo,	Lansing House,	Mass.,	Miscellaneous,	56
Musgrave, Joseph	Eaton,	Charlotte,	"	Penn.,	Banker,	56
Ninde, Thomas	Washtenaw,	Ypsilanti,	"	Maryland,	Lawyer,	51
Norris, Lyman D	Washtenaw,	"	"	New York,	"	43
Parsons, S. Titus	Shiawassee,	Corunna,	"	"	"	40
Pratt, Daniel L	Hillsdale,	Hillsdale,	"	Mass.,	"	46
Pringle, Eugene	Jackson,	Jackson,	Home,	New York,	"	40
Purcell, William	Wayne,	Detroit,	Lansing House,	Ireland,	Moulder,	49
Rafter, William A.†	Monroe,	Monroe,	Vandriss,	Michigan,	Law Student,	26
Richmond, Charles H	Washtenaw,	Ann Arbor,	Lansing House,	New York,	Banker,	45
Root, Simeon P	Hillsdale,	Somerset,	"	"	Physician,	41
Sawyer, Jacob C	Lenawee,	Hudson,	F. Davis,	"	Farmer,	44
Shearer, Jonathan	Wayne,	Plymouth,	Edgar House,	Mass.,	"	72

MEMBERS OF CONVENTION.

Name	County	Town	Hotel/Host	State	Occupation	Age
Sheldon, Horace J.	Lenawee	Blissfield	Geo. Fowler	New York	Shoemaker	54
Smith, Thaddeus G.	Genesee	Fentonville	Lansing House	"	Lawyer	39
Smith, William A.	Wayne	Redford	Edgar House	"	Farmer	51
Stockwell, Martin P.	Lenawee	Dover	F. Davis	"	"	48
Stoughton, William L.	St. Joseph	Sturgis	Lansing House	"	Lawyer	40
Sutherland, Jabez G.	Saginaw	Saginaw	J. Bascom	"	"	41
Thompson, Lewis J.	Hillsdale	North Adams	Mr. Camp		Farmer	53
Turner, Josiah	Shiawassee	Owosso	Lansing House	Vermont	Lawyer	55
Tyler, Comfort	St. Joseph	Oporto	Mrs. Elder	New York	Farmer	66
Utley, William S.	Newaygo	Big Prairie	Mr. Clippenger	"	Lumberman	38
Van Riper, Jacob J.	Cass	Dowagiac	Lansing House	"	Lawyer	29
Van Valkenburgh, Jacob	Oakland	White Lake	American	"	"	72
Walker, Alvah H.	Clinton	St. Johns	Lansing House	R. I.	Merchant	65
Warner, P. Dean	Oakland	Farmington	T. Ford	New York	Miscellaneous	45
Warner, William E.	Wayne	Detroit	Edgar House	"	Register of Deeds	45
Watkins, Milton C.	Kent	Grattan	Dr. Bailey	Vermont	Farmer	61
Watkins, Freeman C.	Jackson	Norvell	Lansing House	N. H.	"	56
White, William E.	Allegan	Wayland	S. R. Greene	New York	Merchant	52
Willard, George	Calhoun	Battle Creek	Lansing House	Vermont	Clergyman	43
Winans, Edwin B.	Livingston	Hamburgh	"	New York	Farmer	40
Winsor, Richard	Huron	Huron City	"	Canada W.	Merchant	29
Withey, Solomon C.	Kent	Grand Rapids	"	Vermont	Lawyer	47
Williams, William B.	Allegan	Allegan	"	"	"	40
Woodhouse, Lemuel	Ingham	Dansville	"	New York	Merchant	47
Wright, Harvey*	Barry	Middleville	"	"	Lawyer	37
Yeomans, Sanford A.	Ionia	Ionia	T. Ford	"	Farmer	50

Secretary, Thos. H. Glenn; Residence, Niles, Berrien Co.; Lodgings, Lansing House.
1st Asst. Secretary, G. X. M. Collier; Residence, Pontiac, Oakland Co.; Lodgings, Lansing House.
2d " T. P. Miles; Residence, St. Clair, St. Clair Co.; Lodgings, Lansing House.
Official Reporter, Wm. Blair Lord; Residence, New York City; Lodgings, Lansing House.
" " David W. Brown; Residence, Philadelphia, Pa.; Lodgings, Lansing House.

LIST OF OFFICERS, &c.—Continued.

Sergeant-at-Arms, D. B. Purinton; Residence, Coldwater, Branch Co.; Lodgings, American.
1st Ass't, " G. L. Montgomery; Residence, Lansing, Ingham Co.; Lodgings, Home.
2d " " H. H. Seaver; Residence, Adrian, Lenawee Co.; Lodgings, American.
Firemen, Bernhardt Rice; Residence, Saginaw, Saginaw Co.; Lodgings, American.
" W. D. Burnham; Residence, Lansing, Ingham Co.; Lodgings, Home.
Pres't's Messenger, Chas. A. Avery; Residence, Adrian, Lenawee Co.; Lodgings, Mr. Carr.
Sec'y's " Wm. H. Porter; Residence, Lansing, Ingham Co.; Lodgings, Mr. Potter.
Messengers, Claude S. Martin; Residence, Dexter, Washtenaw Co.; Lodgings, Mr. Bingham.
" George H. Seymour; Residence, Grand Rapids, Kent Co.; Lodgings, Mr. Carr.
" Chauncey S. Wright; Residence, Fentonville, Genesee Co.; Lodgings, Mr. Carr.
" Willie Elder; Residence, Lansing, Ingham Co.; Lodgings, Home.
" Frederick S. Smith; Residence, Somerset, Hillsdale Co.; Lodgings, Lansing House.
" Cyrus W. Utley; Residence, Big Prairie, Newaygo Co ; Lodgings, Mr. Clippenger.

---

* Widower. † Single. All the rest are married.

RULES OF THE CONVENTION.

RULE I.

The President shall take the Chair at the time to which the Convention stands adjourned, and call it to order; and thereupon the roll of the members shall be called by the Secretary.

RULE II.

Upon the appearance of a quorum, the journal of the preceding day shall be read by the Secretary, unless otherwise ordered, and any mistake therein corrected.

RULE III.

After the reading of the journal of the preceding day, the order of business shall be as follows:
1. Presentation of Petitions.
2. Reports of Standing Committees.
3. Reports of Select Committees.
4. Communications from State Officers.
5. Motions and Resolutions.
6. Third reading of Articles.
7. Unfinished Business.
8. Special Orders of the day.
9. General Orders of the day.

RULE IV.

The President shall preserve order and decorum, and shall decide questions of order, subject to an appeal to the Convention.

RULE V.

The President shall vote upon all questions taken by yeas and nays, except on appeals from his own decisions, in which case he shall not vote.

RULE VI.

The President may leave the Chair and appoint a member to preside, but not for a longer time than one day, except by leave of the Convention.

RULE VII.

When the Convention adjourns, the members shall keep their seats until the President announces the adjournment.

RULE VIII.

Every member, previous to his speaking, shall rise from his seat and address himself to the President.

RULE IX.

When two or more members rise at once, the President shall designate the member who is first to speak.

RULE X.

No member shall speak more than twice on the same question, nor more than once until every member who chooses to speak shall have spoken. This rule shall not apply to chairmen of committees speaking on matters reported by them.

RULE XI.

Every motion shall be reduced to writing, if required by the President or any member, and shall be stated by the President before debate. All resolutions and motions in writing shall be endorsed by the member introducing the same.

RULE XII.

After a motion has been stated by the President, it shall be deemed to be in the possession of the Convention. Such motion may be withdrawn at any time before decision or amendment, but may be renewed by any other member.

RULE XIII.

When a question shall be under debate, no motion shall be received but the following, to wit:

1. To adjourn;
2. To lay on the table;
3. For the previous question;
4. To postpone to a day certain;

5. To commit;
6. To amend;
7. To postpone indefinitely;

Which several motions shall have precedence in the order in which they stand arranged.

RULE XIV.

A motion to adjourn shall always be in order; this, and the motion to lay on the table, shall be decided without debate.

RULE XV.

The previous question shall be in this form: "Shall the main question be now put?" And if demanded by a majority of the members elect, its effect shall be to put an end to all debate, and bring the Convention to a direct vote upon amendments, if any are pending, and then upon the main question, which shall be the section or article under consideration, as the Convention may direct.

RULE XVI.

All incidental questions of order arising after a motion is made for the previous question, during the pendency of such motion, or after the Convention shall have determined that the main question shall now be put, shall be decided, whether on appeal or otherwise, without debate.

RULE XVII.

Petitions, memorials and other papers addressed to the Convention shall be presented by the President or a member in his place, with a brief statement of the contents, and the name of the member presenting the same endorsed thereon.

RULE XVIII.

When the President is putting the question, no member shall walk out of or across the house; nor when a member is speaking, shall any person entertain any private discourse, or pass between him and the Chair.

RULE XIX.

If the question in debate contain several propositions, any member may have the same divided.

RULE XX.

A member called to order by the Chair shall immediately take his seat unless permitted to explain, and the Convention, if appealed to, shall decide the case. If there be no appeal, the decision of the Chair shall be submitted to. On an appeal, no member shall speak more than once without leave of the Convention, and when a member is called to order for offensive language there shall be no debate.

RULE XXI.

When the Convention shall have reached the general orders of the day, they shall go into committee of the whole upon such orders, or a particular order designated by a vote of the Convention; and no other business shall be in order until the whole are considered or passed, or the committee rise; and unless a particular subject is ordered up, the committee of the whole shall consider, act upon, or pass the general orders according to the order of their reference. In forming a committee of the whole, the President shall appoint a chairman to preside.

RULE XXII.

Propositions committed to the committee of the whole shall first be read through by the Secretary, and then read and debated by clauses. All amendments shall be entered on a separate paper, and so reported to the Convention by the chairman, standing in his place.

RULE XXIII.

The rules of the Convention shall be observed in committee of the whole, so far as they may be applicable, except that the yeas and nays shall not be called, nor the previous question enforced. The Convention may at any time, by a vote of the majority of the members present, provide for the discharge of the committee of the whole from the further consideration of any subject referred to it, after acting without debate on all amendments pending, and that may be offered.

RULE XXIV.

A journal of the proceedings in committee of the whole shall be kept as in Convention.

RULE XXV.

A motion that the committee rise shall always be in order, and shall be decided without debate; and if decided in the affirmative, the chairman shall report the action of the committee, either upon the article or section or sections had under consideration, as the committee of the whole shall direct.

RULE XXVI.

All questions, whether in committee or in the Convention, shall be put in the order they were moved, except in the case of privileged questions. Where a blank is to be filled, and different sums or times shall be proposed, the question shall be first taken on the largest sum or the longest time.

RULE XXVII.

No motion for reconsideration shall be in order, unless within three days after the decision proposed to be reconsidered took place. A motion for reconsideration being put and lost, (except in case of privileged motions,) shall not be renewed on the same day.

RULE XXVIII.

Any member having voted with the majority may move a reconsideration, and a motion for reconsideration shall be decided by a majority of votes.

RULE XXIX.

All orders, resolutions and motions shall be entered on the journals of the Convention, with the name of the member moving the same.

RULE XXX.

No rule of the Convention shall be suspended, altered or amended, without the concurrence of two-thirds of the members present.

RULE XXXI.

Upon a call of the Convention, the names of the members shall be called by the Secretary, and the absentees noted; but no excuse shall be made until the Convention shall be fully called over; then the absentees shall be called the second time, and if still absent, excuses may be heard, and if no sufficient excuse be made, the absentees may, by order of those present, if there be fifteen members present, be taken into custody wherever found by the Sergeant-at-Arms.

RULE XXXII.

The rules of parliamentary practice comprised in Jefferson's Manual shall govern the Convention in all cases to which they are applicable, and when they are not inconsistent with the standing rules and orders of this Convention.

RULE XXXIII

The yeas and nays shall be taken upon any question, whenever demanded by ten members, and when so demanded on any question every member within the bar shall vote for or aginst the same, unless the Convention shall excuse him.

RULE XXXIV.

A majority of the members elected shall constitute a quorum for the transaction of business, but a less number may adjourn from day to day.

RULE XXXV.

Every article shall receive three several readings previous to its being passed, and the second and third readings shall be on different days, and the third reading shall be on a day subsequent to that in which it has passed a committee of the whole, unless the Convention, by a vote of two-thirds of the members present, shall otherwise direct; and no article shall be declared adopted without the votes of a majority of all the members elect.

RULE XXXVI.

No article shall be committed or amended until it has been twice read in whole or by its title, as the Convention shall direct; and every article reported upon by a committee shall be referred to the committee of the whole, placed on the general order, and printed.

RULE XXXVII.

When an article shall have reached the order of third reading, it shall be referred to the Committee on Arrangement and Phraseology, for arrangement, correction and engrossment, before it shall be placed upon its final passage.

RULE XXXVIII.

The several articles, after their final passage, shall be referred to the Committee on Arrangement and Phraseology, for numerical arrangement in their proper order, and shall be reported back to the Convention for its final action upon the Constitution as an entirety.

STANDING COMMITTEES.

Boundaries, Seat of Government and the Division of the Powers of Government.

Messrs. LAMB, LONGYEAR, F. C. WATKINS, SHEARER, LEACH.

Legislative Department.

Messrs. CONGER, PRINGLE, PARSONS, LUCE, P. DEAN WARNER, D. GOODWIN, MORTON, M. C. WATKINS, TYLER.

Executive Department.

Messrs. BIRNEY, MUSSEY, VAN VALKENBURGH, MCCLELLAND, CROCKER, LAMB, BROWN.

Judicial Department.

Messrs. WITHEY, TURNER, GIDDINGS, WILLIAMS, DIVINE, PRATT, LOTHROP, SUTHERLAND, NORRIS, HOLT, LOVELL, VAN RIPER, GULICK.

Elections.

Messrs. VAN VALKENBURGH, FERRIS, T. G. SMITH, BURTENSHAW, FARMER, HOLMES, YEOMANS, CROCKER, JENNISON.

State Officers.

Messrs. P. DEAN WARNER, STOUGHTON, INGALLS, GERMAIN, CHAPMAN.

Salaries.

Messrs. MUSSEY, WOODHOUSE, WINSOR, BROWN, HOLMES, DUNCAN, MUSGRAVE, DESNOYERS, McKERNAN.

Counties.

Messrs. LUCE, DIVINE, HENDERSON, STOCKWELL, MILES, WHITE, M. C. WATKINS, HIXSON, LAWRENCE.

Townships.

Messrs. T. G. SMITH, WALKER, BURTCH, SHELDON, W. A. SMITH.

Cities and Villages.

Messrs. MILES, HOLT, MILLER, WRIGHT, WALKER, W. E. WARNER, HENKEL.

Education.

Messrs. WILLARD, LOTHROP, MILLER, CHAPIN, BRADLEY, THOMPSON, HULL, W. F. GOODWIN, RICHMOND.

Finance and Taxation.

Messrs. LEACH, BILLS, McCONNELL, McCLELLAND, RICHMOND, ALEXANDER, MUSGRAVE, HENDERSON, WOODHOUSE.

STANDING COMMITTEES.

Corporations other than Municipal.

Messrs. PRINGLE, BARBER, HAZEN, DUNCAN, SAWYER, ALDRICH, ALEXANDER, W. E. WARNER, RAFTER.

Impeachment.

Messrs. BLACKMAN, HARRIS, HOWARD, MURRAY, W. F. GOODWIN, SAWYER, PURCELL.

Exemptions.

Messrs. COOLIDGE, DANIELLS, LOVELL, HAIRE, RAFTER.

Militia.

Messrs. STOUGHTON, HUSTON, MCCONNELL, KENNY, ANDRUS, CONGER, WINANS.

Miscellaneous Provisions.

Messrs. WILLIAMS, FARMER, BARBER, WITHEY, MCKERNAN.

Amendments and Revisions.

Messrs. GIDDINGS, CHAPIN, HUSTON, ELLIOTT, JENNISON.

Schedule.

Messrs. TURNER, HARRIS, WRIGHT, BURTENSHAW, UTLEY, CASE, BRADLEY, NORRIS, DESNOYERS.

STANDING COMMITTEES.

Arrangement and Phraseology.

Messrs. Ninde, Birney, Coolidge, Blackman, Sutherland, Willard, Daniells.

Bill of Rights.

Messrs. Pratt, Duncombe, Kenny, Van Riper, Andrus, Burtch, Purcell.

Public Lands.

Messrs. Longyear, Hazen, Winsor, Utley, Stockwell, White, Corbin.

Intoxicating Liquors.

Messrs. Bills, Howard, Parsons, Ferris, Ninde, Root, D. Goodwin, Gulick, F. C. Watkins.

Supplies.

Messrs. Aldrich, Case, Root, Haire, Henkel.

Printing.

Messrs. Hull, Ingalls, Morton, Estee, Thompson.

Upper Peninsula.

Messrs. Burtenshaw, Longyear, Conger, McKernan, Gulick.

Crimes and Punishments.

Messrs. Norris, Howard, Yeomans, Murray, Corbin.

POPULATION OF MICHIGAN,
BY COUNTIES.

COUNTIES.	1864.	1860.	1854.	1850.	1845.
Allegan,.............	18,831	16,089	7,804	5,125	2,941
Alpena,,.............	674	290	New	County.	....
Antrim,.............	382	179	Not.Or	ganized.	....
Barry,...............	14,483	14,020	7,821	5,072	2,602
Bay, ...	5,307	3,164	....	556	104
Berrien,.............	25,856	22,323	13,847	11,417	7,365
Branch, ...	22,458	20,410	15,724	12,467	9,064
Calhoun, ...	30,488	31,409	22,768	19,164	15,500
Cass,................	17,776	17,721	13,124	10,897	8,073
Cheboygan,..........	483	517	272	New	County.
Chippewa,...........	1,158	1,603	1,962	898	107
Clinton, ...	14,739	13,926	7,926	5,102	3,010
Delta,................	561	1,172	New	County.	....
Eaton,...............	16,497	15,895	10,965	7,058	3,723
Emmet,..............	1,325	1,149	4,977	New	County.
Genesee,.............	22,776	22,600	15,676	10,955	9,266
Grand Traverse,......	2,017	1,286	517	New	County.
Gratiot,..............	5,831	4,042	116	New	County.
Hillsdale,............	27,324	25,876	19,188	16,159	9,455
Houghton,...........	8,225	5,599	513	126	New Co.
Huron,...............	3,961	3,165	702	207	72
Ingham,..............	17,128	17,531	11,222	8,631	5,240
Ionia,................	17,984	16,682	10,727	7,557	4,940
Iosco,................	495	175	New	County.	....
Isabella,.............	1,844	1,443	New	County.	....
Jackson,.............	25,905	26,671	21,855	19,435	16,826
Kalamazoo,..........	25,824	24,651	16,893	13,179	10,280
Kent, ...	33,458	30,721	17,869	12,016	6,049
Keweenaw,...........	5,180	3,653	2,873	582	....
Lapeer,...............	15,247	14,754	9,704	7,028	5,314
Leelanaw, ...	2,389	2,158	With	Grand T	raverse.
Lenawee,.............	40,202	38,582	31,148	26,372	22,923
Livingston,...........	16,174	16,851	14,185	13,684	10,787
Mackinac,............	1,335	1,938	1,373	3,598	1,666
Macomb, ...	22,404	22,843	18,114	15,530	13,680

POPULATION—Continued.

COUNTIES.	1864.	1860.	1854.	1850.	1845.
Manistee,	1,673	975	394	New County.	
Manitou,		1,043	New County.		
Marquette,	3,724	2,821		136	
Mason,	844	831			
Mecosta,	1,382	880	New County.		
Menominee,	496				
Midland,	1,244	787		65	
Monroe,	22,221	21,596	18,122	14,698	13,287
Montcalm,	5,619	3,968	2,060	891	161
Muskegon,	5,812	3,947	1,335	752	217
Newaygo,	3,481	2,760	979	510	New Co.
Oakland,	33,735	37,720	31,884	31,279	30,245
Oceana,	2,379	1,816		300	New Co.
Ontonagon,	5,406	3,973	3,662	389	New Co.
Ottawa,	15,156	13,215	7,137	4,492	1,253
Saginaw,	19,682	12,693	1,053	2,063	920
Sanilac,	8,853	7,599	3,529	2,112	868
Shiawassee,	13,465	12,359	7,419	5,229	3,862
St. Clair,	27,591	26,750	16,897	9,953	6,622
St. Joseph,	21,796	21,108	15,087	12,725	10,097
Tuscola,	6,983	4,886	1,504	291	104
Van Buren,	17,830	15,224	8,300	5,760	3,865
Washtenaw,	34,048	35,659	28,836	28,475	26,776
Wayne,	83,326	74,727	65,778	42,756	29,225
Unorganized Counties,	1,195	330		16	
Total,	805,379	748,645	513,893	395,697	296,487

AGGREGATE OF REAL AND PERSONAL ESTATE IN MICHIGAN,

As Assessed and Equalized by the Boards of Supervisors and the State Board of Equalization.

COUNTIES.	Aggregate of Real and Personal Estate as equalized by Board, 1851.	Aggregate of Real and Personal Estate as assessed, 1853.	Aggregate of Real and Personal Estate as equalized by Board Supervisors, 1853.	Amount added or deducted by State Board.	Aggregate of Real and Personal Estate as equalized by State Board, 1853.
Allegan,	$488,077 90	$1,541,737 43	$1,541,737 43	Ded. $200,000 00	$1,341,737 43
Alpena,					
Antrim,					
Barry,	409,769 00	1,210,484 55	1,224,587 95		1,224,587 95
Bay,					
Berrien,	775,038 31	3,022,658 00	3,060,883 55		3,060,883 55
Branch,	837,289 15	3,188,308 00	2,874,354 00	Add 863,954 00	3,738,308 00
Calhoun,	1,637,347 00	3,742,270 00	3,646,946 00	Add 1,783,758 00	5,430,704 00
Cass,	841,411 00	2,710,660 00	2,700,660 00	Add 244,278 00	2,944,938 00
Cheboygan,					

EQUALIZATION OF PROPERTY. 41

Chippewa,	105,291 00		200,000 00
Clinton,	382,783 00	1,174,323 00	1,164,959 00	1,164,959 00
Delta,			
Eaton,	519,614 52	1,692,927 00	1,732,854 00	1,732,854 00
Emmet,			
Genesee,	735,209 23	2,980,9?4 54	Add 566,319 46 2,548,036 54	3,114,356 00
Grand Traverse,			
Gratiot,			
Hillsdale,	993,240 00	4,169,523 76	Ded. 157,702 76 4,167,225 76	4,009,523 00
Houghton,			
Huron,			
Ingham,	588,387 00	1,870,153 00	1,853,000 00	1,853,000 00
Ionia,	515,993 67	1,938,130 50	2,007,218 87	2,007,218 87
Iosco,			
Isabella,			
Jackson,	1,516,459 01	5,758,013 00	5,723,798 00	5,723,798 00
Kalamazoo,	1,098,192 15	4,787,874 00	4,810,655 00	4,810,655 00

6

AGGREGATE OF REAL AND PERSONAL ESTATE—Continued.

COUNTIES.	Aggregate of Real and Personal Estate as equalized by Board, 1851.	Aggregate of Real and Personal Estate as assessed, 1853.	Aggregate of Real and Personal Estate as equalized by Board Supervisors, 1853.	Amount added or deducted by State Board.	Aggregate of Real and Personal Estate as equalized by State Board, 1853.
Kent,	$883,014 78	$3,734,440 00	$3,562,823 00		$3,562,823 00
Keweenaw,					
Lapeer,	406,400 88	1,771,019 33	1,666,118 59		1,666,118 59
Leelanaw,					
Lenawee,	2,358,059 82	9,590,431 00	9,609,813 00		9,609,813 00
Livingston,	807,687 20	2,738,576 86	3,278,626 97	Ded. $200,000 00	3,078,626 97
Mackinac,	127,709 70	169,902 25	169,902 25		169,902 25
Macomb,	896,246 00	4,366,309 00	4,510,399 00	Ded. 500,000 00	4,010,399 00
Manistee,					
Manitou,					
Marquette,					

EQUALIZATION OF PROPERTY. 43

Mason,						
Mecosta,						
Menominee,						
Midland,						
Monroe,	960,344 22	3,843,595 00		3,811,875 00		3,811,875 00
Montcalm,	109,182 55	265,422 00		291,645 00		291,645 00
Muskegon,						
Newaygo,		153,928 75		153,928 75		153,928 75
Oakland,	2,441,475 74	8,618,290 00		8,617,930 00		8,617,930 00
Oceana,						
Ontonagon,						
Ottawa,	481,847 23	1,239,114 25		1,322,479 70		1,322,479 70
Saginaw,	357,973 01	1,327,393 49		1,336,002 22		1,333,002 22
Sanilac,	221,225 19	776,657 00		776,657 00		776,657 00
Shiawassee,	411,666 49	1,155,017 00		1,280,488 00		1,280,488 00
St. Clair,	977,261 25	3,325,076 02		3,052,532 39	Add 856,511 61	3,909,044 00
St. Joseph,	1,088,923 00	4,104,713 00		4,116,975 00		4,116,975 00

AGGREGATE OF REAL AND PERSONAL ESTATE—Continued.

COUNTIES.	Aggregate of Real and Personal Estate as equalized by Board, 1851.	Aggregate of Real and Personal Estate as assessed, 1853.	Aggregate of Real and Personal Estate as equalized by Board Supervisors, 1853.	Amount added or deducted by State Board.	Aggregate of Real and Personal Estate as equalized by State Board, 1853.
Tuscola,.........	$115,249 58	$281,122 43	$278,157 93	....	$278,157 93
Van Buren,.......	541,663 35	1,482,757 79	1,683,561 14	....	1,683,561 14
Washtenaw,......	2,517,427 00	9,012,392 00	9,375,000 00	....	9,375,000 00
Wayne,...........	3,833,213 76	17,953,525 00	16,097,331 30	Add 2,856,193 70	18,953,525 00
Totals,...........	$30,976,270 18	$115,647,758 95	$114,049,162 34	....	$120,362,404 35

AGGREGATE OF REAL AND PERSONAL ESTATE IN MICHIGAN,

As Assessed and Equalized by the Boards of Supervisors and the State Board of Equalization.

COUNTIES.	No. of acres of Land assessed in 1861.	Aggregate of Real and Personal Estate, as assessed in 1861.	Aggregate of Real and Personal Estate as equalized by Board Supervisors.	Amount added or deducted by State Board of Equalization.	Aggregate of Real and Personal Estate as equalized by State Board of Equalization.
Allegan,	493,761.00	$3,061,876 00	$2,998,876 00	Ded. $18,551 00	$2,980,325 00
Alpena,	237,832.02	367,362 78	367,362 78	....	367,362 78
Antrim,	....	....	....	....	....
Barry,	347,747.00	1,757,797 00	1,743,642 00	Add 397,078 00	2,140,720 00
Bay,	142,078.00	697,426 00	635,309 00	Add 40,553 00	675,862 00
Berrien,	355,087.00	4,676,268 00	4,222,042 00	Add 323,820 00	4,545,862 00
Branch,	316,793.00	3,805,903 00	3,802,948 00	Add 1,100,000 00	4,902,948 00
Calhoun,	438,542.37	5,081,784 00	5,819,358 00	Add 1,264,542 00	7,083,900 00
Cass,	302,871.00	3,813,881 00	3,813,881 00	Add 100,000 00	3,913,881 00
Cheboygan,	22,170.00	83,686 20	77,225 20	....	77,225 20

AGGREGATE OF REAL AND PERSONAL ESTATE—Continued.

COUNTIES.	Number of acres of Land assessed in 1861.	Aggregate of Real and Personal Estate as assessed in 1861.	Aggregate of Real and Personal Estate as equalized by Board Supervisors.	Amount added or deducted by State Board of Equalization.		Aggregate of Real and Personal Estate as equalized by State Board of Equalization.
Chippewa,......	20,070.03	$111,224 36	$111,824 36	Ded.	$111,224 36	$100,000 00
Clinton,........	346,550.63	2,406,314 00	1,977,538 00	Add	385,802 00	2,363,340 00
Delta,..........	....	....	....	....	....	150,000 00
Eaton,..........	350,679.00	3,201,910 00	3,046,828 00	Ded.	253,513 00	2,792,315 00
Emmet,.........	5,913.64	41,102 36	41,102 36	....	....	41,102 36
Genesee,........	395,342.00	4,056,830 00	4,052,298 00	Ded.	26,368 00	4,025,930 00
Grand Traverse,..	164,661.00	521,298 00	498,459 00	Add	50,000 00	548,459 00
Gratiot,........	274,602.00	787,372 00	595,711 00	Add	12,150 00	607,861 00
Hillsdale,.......	379,202.00	5,407,782 00	5,252,637 00	Add	993,714 00	6,246,351 00
Houghton,......	134,869.02	1,033,666 72	1,033,666 72	Ded.	33,236 72	1,000,430 00
Huron,..........	185,406.00	533,591 16	466,855 00	Add	78,455 00	545,310 00

EQUALIZATION OF PROPERTY. 47

Ingham,	333,497.00	$2,910,247 00	$2,748,990 00		$2,748,990 00
Ionia,	343,828.50	3,376,465 25	3,356,875 25	Ded. $316,356 25	3,040,519 00
Iosco,	83,283.30	129,250 37	129,250 37		129,250 37
Isabella,	134,727.00	497,080 00	457,080 00	Ded. 73,411 00	383,669 00
Jackson,	432,158.00	6,476,813 00	5,034,559 00	Add 2,018,121 00	7,052,680 00
Kalamazoo,	346,255.00	4,646,911 00	4,689,662 00	Add 1,100,000 00	5,789,662 00
Kent,	516,425.00	6,357,454 00	6,431,679 00	Add 1,764,609 00	8,196,288 00
Keweenaw,	118,425.95⅔	771,032 02	771,032 02		771,032 02
Lapeer,	392,626.80	2,286,622 00	2,137,307 00		2,137,307 00
Leelanaw,					
Lenawee,	465,446.00	10,360,157 00	10,288,929 00	Add 1,077,111 00	11,366,040 00
Livingston,	365,472.92	3,156,530 00	3,155,430 00	Ded. 155,230 00	3,000,200 00
Mackinac,	30,975.77	147,785 00	147,785 00		147,785 00
Macomb,	295,845.00	4,899,459 00	4,809,959 00		4,809,959 00
Manistee,	99,043.35	338,662 62	335,662 62		335,662 62
Manitou,	9,388.00	62,177 00	62,177 00		62,177 00
Marquette,					1,000,000 00

AGGREGATE OF REAL AND PERSONAL ESTATE—Continued.

COUNTIES.	Number of acres of Land assessed in 1861.	Aggregate of Real and Personal Estate as assessed in 1861.	Aggregate of Real and Personal Estate as exualized by Board Supervisors.	Amount added or deducted by State Board of Equalization.		Aggregate of Real and Personal Estate as equalized by State Board of Equalization.
Mason,	83,261.76	$212,897 40	$178,133 82	Add	$75,737 18	$253,871 00
Mecosta,	235,876.28	342,410 15	342,410 15	Add	130,089 85	472,500 00
Menominee,						154,000 00
Midland,	280,090.14	583,520 76	572,385 96	Add	11,134 04	583,520 00
Monroe,	333,904.00	4,071,835 00	4,061,383 00	Add	200,000 00	4,261,383 00
Montcalm,	315,742.38	1,037,162 00	1,037,107 00	Ded.	100,000 00	937,107 00
Muskegon,	150,681.14	793,884 52	860,524 12			860,524 12
Newaygo,	250,316.26	703,911 00	675,412 00	Add	100,000 00	775,412 00
Oakland,	539,590.00	9,689,543 00	9,689,543 00	Add	1,533,677 00	11,223,220 00
Oceana,	166,278.10	427,054 59	424,943 95	Ded.	62,943 95	362,000 00
Ontonagon,	193,009.50	1,132,329 00	1,132,329 00	Ded.	479,007 00	653,322 00

EQUALIZATION OF PROPERTY.

Ottawa,........	294,025.18	$1,353,723 00	$1,374,317 00	Add $502,503 00	$1,876,820 00
Saginaw,.......	420,679.00	2,480,487 60	2,250,424 63	Add 243,235 37	2,493,600 00
Sanilac,........	403,292.90	1,520,274 14	1,513,158 34	Ded. 21,350 34	1,491,808 00
Shiawassee,....	341,427.02	2,672,644 00	2,466,282 00	Add 100,000 00	2,566,282 00
St. Clair,.......	424,325.00	3,607,428 00	3,575,391 00	Add 421,449 00	3,996,840 00
St. Joseph,.....	314,322.73	5,800,059 00	5,825,565 00	....	5,825,565 00
Tuscola, ...	341,245.49	1,118,891 69	930,709 42	....	930,709 42
Van Buren,.....	381,723.22	2,587,654 00	2,365,650 00	Add 225,840 00	2,591,490 00
Washtenaw,....	429,832.00	9,253,558 00	8,900,000 00	Add 1,260,430 00	10,160,430 00
Wayne,.........	380,714.00	20,010,220 00	18,582,982 00	Add 4,920,958 00	23,503,940 00
Totals,........	15,162,710.40¾	$157,863,206 69	$151,871,992 07	....	$172,055,808 89

AGGREGATE OF REAL AND PERSONAL ESTATE IN MICHIGAN,

As Assessed and Equalized by the Boards of Supervisors and the State Board of Equalization.

COUNTIES.	Number of acres of Land assessed 1856.	Aggregate of Real and Personal Estate as assessed, 1856.	Aggregate of Real and Personal Estate as equalized by Boards of Supervisors.	Amount added or deducted by State Board of Equalization.		Aggregate of Real and Personal Estate as equalized by State Board of Equalization.
Allegan,........	464,979.00	$1,704,698 00	$2,704,798 00	Ded.	$197,527 00	$2,507,271 00
Alpena,........	....	....	....	....	....	....
Antrim,........	....	....	....	....	....	....
Barry,.........	232,550.00	1,720,339 00	1,710,948 00	Add	69,052 00	1,780,000 00
Bay,...........	....	....	....	....	....	....
Berrien,........	350,515.00	4,245,357 00	4,426,061 90	Ded.	486,866 00	3,939,195 00
Branch,........	312,696.00	3,796,734 00	3,799,317 00	Add	27,076 00	3,828,393 00
Calhoun,.......	438,188.85	5,426,584 00	5,426,584 00	Add	26,112 00	5,452,660 00
Cass,...........	297,875.79	3,703,478 00	3,703,478 00	Ded.	407,382 00	3,296,096 00
Cheboygan,.....	6,450.66	89,289 25	90,115 00	Ded.	9,912 00	80,203 00

EQUALIZATION OF PROPERTY.

County					
Chippewa,					100,000 00
Clinton,	334,275.00	2,174,123 00		239,813 00	1,940,310 00
Delta,					
Eaton,	338,546.00	3,135,767 00	Ded.	553,123 00	2,225,000 00
Emmet,					50,000 00
Genesee,	388,775.00	3,922,987 00	Ded.		4,013,455 00
Grand Traverse,			Add	4,956 00	160,000 00
Gratiot,	224,929.00	585,847 00		474,191 00	
Hillsdale,	379,017.28	5,171,400 00	Ded.	118,191 00	356,000 00
Houghton,			Ded.	567,864 00	4,594,536 00
Huron,					300,000 00
Ingham,	333,374.05	2,894,810 55			
Ionia,	338,095.22	3,189,605 25	Ded.	611,811 55	2,314,000 00
Iosco,			Ded.	830,528 00	2,314,000 00
Isabella,					
Jackson,	435,677.00	6,526,113 00	Ded.	681,991 00	5,517,934 00
Kalamazoo,	346,246.00	5,781,582 00	Ded.	618,115 00	5,001,114 00

AGGREGATE OF REAL AND PERSONAL ESTATE—Continued.

COUNTIES.	Number of acres of Land assessed 1856.	Aggregate of Real and Personal Estate as assessed, 1856.	Aggregate of Real and Personal Estate as equalized by Boards of Supervisors.	Amount added or deducted by State Board of Equalization.	Aggregate of Real and Personal Estate as equalized by State Board of Equalization.
Kent,	506,136.24	$6,503,338 18	$6,557,737 50	Ded. $721,351 50	$5,833,386 00
Keweenaw,	....	....	....	....	....
Lapeer,	372,869.96	2,256,841 00	2,199,141 00	Ded. 241,905 00	1,957,236 00
Leelanaw,	....	....	....	....	....
Lenawee,	....	10,674,746 00	10,536,619 00	Ded. 1,159,028 00	9,377,591 00
Livingston,	258,004.43	3,296,369 75	3,238,357 00	Ded. 356,219 00	2,882,135 00
Mackinac,	3,181.48	154,331 00	165,599 00	Ded. 18,215 00	147,384 00
Macomb,	189,270.00	5,296,466 00	5,296,466 00	Ded. 582,511 00	4,713,955 00
Manistee,	40,660.94	....	221,531 44	Ded. 24,368 44	197,163 00
Manitou,	....	....	....	....	25,000 00
Marquette,	....	....	....	....	325,000 00

EQUALIZATION OF PROPERTY.

County						
Mason,						50,000 00
Mescosta,						
Menominee,						
Midland,	201,103 79	560,600 66	569,514 80	Ded.	62,646 80	506,868 00
Monroe,	330,728 00	4,236,159 00	4,199,570 00	Ded.	461,952 00	3,737,618 00
Montcalm,	219,689 00	893,580 00	893,581 00	Ded.	98,293 00	795,288 00
Muskegon,						
Newaygo,	201,000 00	702,286 00	647,225 00	Ded.	71,194 00	575,031 00
Oakland,	513,994 00	10,266,760 00	10,266,760 00	Ded.	1,129,343 00	9,137,417 00
Oceana,	54,428 84	209,292 62	232,994 62	Ded.	25,628 62	207,366 00
Ontonagon,	201,862 54		511,169 88	Add	22,880 12	534,000 00
Ottawa,	393,344 46	2,363,729 21	2,438,437 15	Ded.	268,228 15	2,170,209 00
Saginaw,	456,081 03	2,520,803 86	2,511,121 62	Ded.	276,223 62	2,234,898 00
Sanilac,	401,327 26	1,729,033 87	1,740,864 44	Ded.	191,939 44	1,548,925 00
Shiawassee,	318,547 00	2,229,656 00	2,459,248 00	Ded.	270,627 00	2,189,621 00
St. Clair,	395,017 50	3,753,860 00	3,767,672 15	Ded.	414,443 15	3,353,229 00
St. Joseph,	311,202 44	5,273,170 00	5,412,958 00	Ded.	962,958 00	4,450,000 00

AGGREGATE OF REAL AND PERSONAL ESTATE—Continued.

COUNTIES.	Number of acres of Land assessed 1856.	Aggregate of Real and Personal Estate as assessed, 1856.	Aggregate of Real and Personal Estate as equalized by Boards of Supervisors.	Amount added or deducted by State Board of Equalization.	Aggregate of Real and Personal Estate as equalized by State Board of Equalization.
Tuscola,	279,163.34	$927,026 79	$922,094 45	Ded. $101,430 45	$820,664 00
Van Buren,	369,406.58	2,402,243 75	2,395,925 94	Ded. 263,551 94	2,132,374 00
Washtenaw,	440,931.16	9,194,680 00	9,000,000 00	Ded. 100,000 00	8,900,000 00
Wayne,	382,762.00	20,236,936 00	19,148,481 00	....	19,148,481 00
Totals,	12,167,812.84	$149,749,623 41	$149,688,200 44	....	$137,663,009 00

AGGREGATE OF REAL AND PERSONAL ESTATE IN MICHIGAN,

As Assessed and Equalized by the Boards of Supervisors and the State Board of Equalization.

COUNTIES.	Number of acres of Land assessed in 1866.	Aggregate of Real and Personal Estate, as assessed in 1866.	Aggregate of Real and Personal Estate as equalized by Boards of Supervisors.	Amount added or deducted by State Board of Equalization.	Aggregate of Real and Personal Estate as equalized by State Board of Equalization, 1866.
Allegan,........	496,043.00	$3,183,816 00	$3,077,307 00	Add 2,867,474 66	$5,941,781 66
Alpena,........	349,255.26	1,299,284 36	1,299,284 36	Add 448,563 96	1,747,848 32
Antrim,........	129,515.99	218,023 53	206,636 61	Add 537,791 71	534,428 32
Barry,.........	343,054.00	1,864,958 00	1,857,815 00	Add 1,529,993 32	3,387,808 22
Bay,...........	193,715.89	1,457,708 00	1,448,790 00	Add 1,053,193 32	2,501,983 32
Berrien,........	349,426.46	4,620,010 00	5,257,735 00	Add 2,843,726 66	8,101,461 66
Branch,........	311,867.00	4,055,296 00	4,038,260 00	Add 2,961,713 32	6,999,973 32
Calhoun,.......	443,770.00	6,167,774 00	6,167,774 00	Add 6,190,894 32	12,338,668 32
Cass,..........	309,850.00	4,003,755 00	3,988,000 00	Add 3,091,051 66	7,079,051 66
Cheboygan,.....	31,968.00	84,128 00	79,128 00	Add 73,733 66	152,861 66

AGGREGATE OF REAL AND PERSONAL ESTATE—Continued.

COUNTIES.	Number of acres of Land assessed in 1866.	Aggregate of Real and Personal Estate, as assessed in 1866.	Aggregate of Real and Personal Estate as equalized by Boards of Supervisors.	Amount added or deducted by State Board of Equalization.	Aggregate of Real and Personal Estate as equalized by State Board of Equalization, 1866.
Chippewa,	30,640.18	$125,905 00	$125,905 00	Add $42,550 00	$168,455 00
Clinton,	349,845.92	2,676,817 44	2,676,817 44	Add 1,520,400 88	4,197,218 32
Delta,	....	....	....	....	256,650 00
Eaton	358,608.00	3,164,512 00	3,092,860 00	Add 1,375,000 00	4,467,860 00
Emmet,	21,994.09	61,876 87	62,790 12	Add 53,981 54	116,771 66
Genesee,	392,991.00	4,387,699 00	4,464,737 00	Add 3,281,541 32	7,746,278 32
Grand Traverse,	139,448.26	313,287 00	311,723 00	Add 387,378 66	699,101 66
Gratiot,	289,718.00	930,533 00	711,259 00	Add 923,486 00	1,634,745 00
Hillsdale,	277,322.23	6,013,013 00	5,791,041 00	Add 3,212,845 66	9,003,806 66
Houghton,	284,629.66	2,047,922 13	1,865,000 00	Add 1,377,523 32	3,242,523 32
Huron,	250,750.00	723,624 91	737,610 61	Add 573,266 05	1,310,776 66

EQUALIZATION OF PROPERTY.   57

Ingham,........	340,468.00	$3,147,872 00		$2,863,000 00	Add 1,606,960 00	$4,469,960 00
Ionia,.........	360,320.52	3,922,548 00		3,965,370 00	Add 2,842,578 32	6,807,948 32
Iosco,.........	257,387.88	633,273 81		633,273 81	Add 510,849 51	1,144,133 32
Isabella,.......	242,777.49	664,445 49		535,426 61	Add 536,398 39	1,071,825 00
Jackson,.......	433,700.00	6,858,880 00		6,067,086 00	Add 6,651,485 66	12,718,571 66
Kalamazoo,....	340,035.00	5,576,204 00		5,619,443 00	Add 4,356,903 66	9,976,346 66
Kent,..........	520,401.00	7,022,318 00		6,733,968 00	Add 5,149,677 00	11,883,645 00
Keweenaw,.....	248,629.38	1,703,846 20		1,409,700 20	Add 1,102,473 12	2,512,173 32
Lapeer,........	414,274.14	2,268,082 00		2,216,010 00	Add 2,499,721 66	4,715,731 66
Leelanaw,......	60,193.91	227,554 00		231,564 00	Add 99,047 66	330,611 66
Lenawee,......	468,382 00	10,724,100 00		10,286,178 00	Add 7,273,065 32	17,559,343 32
Livingston,.....	364,210.00	3,245,041 00		2,875,881 00	Add 3,388,554 00	6,264,435 00
Mackinac,.....	30,487.23	237,917 15		237,917 15	Add 135,707 85	373,625 00
Macomb,......	295,580.00	5,193,249 00		5,273,249 00	Add 3,336,934 32	8,610,183 32
Manistee,......	138,041.44	612,826 91		612,826 91	Add 200,431 41	813,258 32
Manitou,.......	20,989.41	117,306 00		117,306 00	Add 33,215 66	150,521 66
Marquette,.....	280,569.48	1,139,989 00		1,128,794 00	Add 1,118,611 00	2,247,405 00

AGGREGATE OF REAL AND PERSONAL ESTATE—Continued.

COUNTIES.	Number of acres of Land assessed in 1866.	Aggregate of Real and Personal Estate, as assessed in 1866.	Aggregate of Real and Personal Estate as equalized by Boards of Supervisors.	Amount added or deducted by State Board of Equalization.		Aggregate of Real and Personal Estate as equalized by State Board of Equalization, 1866.
Mason,	101,664.95	$239,188 42	$238,889 00	Add	$247,086 00	$485,975 00
Mecosta,	276,464.37	769,954 10	775,040 50	Add	438,434 50	1,213,475 00
Menominee,	91,981.00	241,728 00	241,728 00	Add	198,532 00	440,260 00
Midland,	449,136.91	1,326,243 00	1,326,243 00	Add	554,988 66	1,881,231 66
Monroe,	337,326.00	4,281,928 00	4,271,610 55	Add	2,630,191 11	6,901,801 66
Montcalm,	350,431.00	1,230,491 00	1,175,231 00	Add	865,605 66	2,040,836 66
Muskegon,	190,715.09	1,634,747 72	1,623,689 39	Add	1,019,417 27	2,643,106 66
Newaygo,	273,218.59	949,174 00	948,265 18	Add	632,176 48	1,580,441 66
Oakland,	478,261.39	9,066,705 00	9,066,705 00	Add	6,321,855 00	15,388,560 00
Oceana,	200,600.65	575,690 69	610,861 13	Add	353,478 87	964,340 80
Ontonagon,	191,521.33	865,128 58	677,457 58	Add	743,927 42	1,421,385 00

EQUALIZATION OF PROPERTY. 59

Ottawa,	314,984.00	1,870,761 00	1,832,122 00 Add 1,671,071 32	3,503,193 31
Saginaw,	457,177.07	3,487,419 55	3,875,576 67 Add 4,583,715 99	8,459,291 66
Sanilac,	497,021.61	1,578,501 00	1,532,984 00 Add 945,419 32	2,478,403 32
Shiawassee,	333,588.77	2,248,774 00	2,119,565 00 Add 1,667,786 66	3,787,351 65
St. Clair,	426,446.00	3,783,919 00	3,783,919 00 Add 2,522,612 66	6,306,531 66
St. Joseph,	303,531.00	6,396,603 00	6,343,536 00 Add 2,886,205 66	9,229,741 66
Tuscola,	383,572.00	1,406,023 00	1,433,593 00 Add 988,860 32	2,422,453 32
Van Buren,	380,828.60	3,415,697 00	3,025,000 00 Add 1,901,238 32	4,926,238 32
Washtenaw,	429,454.00	9,747,064 00	10,000,000 00 Add 7,189,765 00	17,189,765 00
Wayne,	371,027.26	23,245,285 00	23,239,561 00 " 18,132,157 32	41,371,708 32
Totals,	17,111,710.91	$179,065,460 86	$176,209,042 82	$307,965,842 92

SUPREME COURT.

CHIEF JUSTICE,
GEO. MARTIN; Residence, Grand Rapids.

ASSOCIATE JUSTICES,
ISAAC P. CHRISTIANCY; Residence, Monroe.
JAMES V. CAMPBELL; Residence, Detroit.
THOMAS M. COOLEY; Residence, Ann Arbor.

CIRCUIT COURTS.

1st *Circuit*—Monroe, Lenawee and Hillsdale. Judge—FRANKLIN JOHNSON, Monroe.

2d *Circuit*—Branch, St. Joseph, Cass and Berrien. Judge—NATHANIEL BACON, Niles.

3d *Circuit*—Wayne, Emmet and Cheboygan. Judge—CHARLES I. WALKER, Detroit.

4th *Circuit*—Washtenaw, Jackson and Ingham. Judge—EDWIN LAWRENCE, Ann Arbor.

5th *Circuit*—Calhoun and Eaton. Judge—GEORGE WOODRUFF, Marshall.

6th *Circuit*—St. Clair, Macomb, Oakland and Sanilac. Judge—JAMES S. DEWEY, Pontiac.

7th Circuit—Livingston, Shiawassee, Genesee, Lapeer and Tuscola. Judge—JOSIAH TURNER, Owosso.

8th Circuit—Ionia, Clinton, Kent, Montcalm and Barry. Judge—LOUIS S. LOVELL, Ionia.

9th Circuit—Allegan, Kalamazoo and Van Buren. Judge—FLAVIUS J. LITTLEJOHN, Allegan.

10th *Circuit*—Saginaw, Gratiot, Isabella, Midland, Iosco, Bay and Alpena; and the following unorganized Counties are attached for Judicial and Municipal purposes, and form a part of said Circuit—to the County of Midland are attached the Counties of Gladwin, Clare and Roscommon; and to the County of Alpena, the Counties of Montmorenci, Presque Isle, Oscoda and Alcona. Judge—JABEZ G. SUTHERLAND, Saginaw.

11*th Circuit*—Mackinac, Chippewa, Delta and Menominee. Judge—D. GOODWIN, Detroit.

12*th Circuit*—Ontonagon, Keweenaw, Houghton and Marquette. Judge—CLARENCE E. EDDIE, Houghton, L. S.

13*th Circuit*—Mason, Manistee, Wexford, Missaukee, Benzie, Grand Traverse, Kalkaska, Leelanaw, Antrim, Otsego and Manitou. Judge —J. G. RAMSDELL, Traverse City.

14*th Circuit*—Ottawa, Newaygo, Oceana, Muskegon and Mecosta. Judge—MOSES B. HOPKINS, Grand Haven.

GOVERNORS OF MICHIGAN TERRITORY.

WILLIAM HULL,	1805
LEWIS CASS,	1814
GEORGE B. PORTER,	1829
STEVENS T. MASON,	1834
J. T. HORNER, *Ex Officio*,	1835

GOVERNORS OF THE STATE OF MICHIGAN.

STEVENS T. MASON,	1835–6
WM. WOODBRIDGE,	1840
J. W. GORDON, (Acting,)	1841
JOHN S. BARRY,	1842
ALPHEUS FELCH,	1846
WM. N. GREENLY, (Acting,)	1847
EPAPHRODITUS RANSOM,	1848
JOHN S. BARRY,	1850
ROBERT McCLELLAND,	1852
ANDREW PARSONS, (Acting,)	1853
KINSLEY S. BINGHAM,	1855
MOSES WISNER,	1859
AUSTIN BLAIR,	1861
AUSTIN BLAIR,	1863
HENRY H. CRAPO,	1865
HENRY H. CRAPO,	1867

A LIST OF U. S. SENATORS FROM MICHIGAN.

LUCIUS LYON, ... 1836–40
JOHN NORVELL, ... 1836–41
AUGUSTUS A. PORTER, ... 1840–45
WILLIAM WOODBRIDGE, ... 1841–47
LEWIS CASS, ... 1845–48
THOS. H. FITZGERALD, ... 1848–49
LEWIS CASS, ... 1849–57
ALPHEUS FELCH, ... 1847–53
CHARLES E. STUART, ... 1853–59
ZACHARIAH CHANDLER, ... 1857–69
KINSLEY S. BINGHAM, ... 1859–61
JACOB M. HOWARD, ... 1862–71

REPRESENTATIVES IN CONGRESS FROM MICH.

ISAAC E. CRARY, ... 1836–41
JACOB M. HOWARD, ... 1841–43
LUCIUS LYON, ... 1843–45
ROBERT McCLELLAND, ... 1843–47
JAMES B. HUNT, ... 1843–47
JOHN S. CHIPMAN, ... 1845–47
ROBERT McCLELLAND, ... 1847–49
CHARLES E. STUART, ... 1847–49
KINSLEY S. BINGHAM, ... 1849–51
ALEXANDER W. BUEL, ... 1849–51
WILLIAM SPRAGUE, ... 1849–51

REPRESENTATIVES IN CONGRESS. 65

JAMES L. CONGER,...............1851-53
CHARLES E. STUART,............1851-53
EBENEZER J. PENNIMAN,........1851-53
SAMUEL CLARK,.................1853-55
DAVID A. NOBLE,................1853-55
HESTOR L. STEVENS,.............1853-55
DAVID STUART,..................1853-55
GEORGE W. PECK,...............1855-57
WM. A. HOWARD,................1855-57
HENRY WALDRON,...............1855-57
DAVID S. WALBRIDGE,..........1855-57
WM. A. HOWARD,................1857-59
DAVID S. WALBRIDGE,..........1857-59
HENRY WALDRON,..............1857-59
D. C. LEACH,....................1857 59
WM. A. HOWARD, ...1859-61
HENRY WALDRON,..............1859-61
D. C. LEACH,....................1859-61
FRANCIS W. KELLOGG,..........1859-61
B. F. GRANGER,..................1861-63
F. C. BEAMAN,...................1861-63
F. W. KELLOGG,.................1861-63
ROWLAND E. TROWBRIDGE,.....1861-63
CHARLES UPSON,................1863-65
F. C. BEAMAN,....................1863-65
JOHN W. LONGYEAR,............1863-65
F. W. KELLOGG,..................1863-65
A. C. BALDWIN,........ 1863-65
JOHN F. DRIGGS,.................1863-65
JOHN. W. LONGYEAR,............1865-67

CHARLES UPSON,.................1865-67
JOHN F. DRIGGS,..................1865-67
THOS. W. FERRY,.................1865-67
ROWLAND E. TROWBRIDGE,....1865-67
F. C. BEAMAN,....................1865-67
JOHN F. DRIGGS,.................1867-69
CHARLES UPSON,................1867-69
THOS. W. FERRY,.................1867-69
ROWLAND E. TROWBRIDGE,....1867-69
F. C. BEAMAN,....................1867-69
AUSTIN BLAIR,....................1867-69

NAMES OF DELEGATES IN THE CONSTITUTIONAL CONVENTION OF 1835.

ADAM, JOHN J.
AXFORD, JOHN S.
AXFORD, SAMUEL
BARRY, JOHN S.
BEAUFAIT, LEWIS
BIDDLE, JOHN
BOUGHTON, SELLECK C.
BREWER, JOHN
BRIGGS, RUSSELL
BROWN, AMMON
BROWN, RICHARD
CASE, EMANUEL
CALKIN, EPHRAIM
CHAPMAN, BELA
CLARK, ELIPHALET
CLARKE, JOHN
CHASE, JONATHAN
COLBATH, LEMUEL
COLLINS, ALPHEUS
COMSTOCK, DARIUS
CONVIS, EZRA
COOK, ELIJAH
CROSSMAN, RUFUS
CURTIS, THOMAS

CRARY, ISAAC E.
DAVIS, J. D.
DAVISON, NORMAN
DOUSMAN, MICHAEL
ELLENWOOD, JOHN
ELLIS, EDWARD D.
FERRINGTON, CALEB
FERRY, PETER P.
GIDLEY, TOWNSEND E.
GODARD, ABEL
GODFROY, JAMES J.
HERRINGTON, CALEB
HOWE, ORIN
HOWELL, JOSEPH Jr.
HUTCHINS, ALLEN
INGERSOLL, SAMUEL
IRWIN, CHARLES F.
JENKINS, BALDWIN
LACY, ELIJAH
LOOMIS, HUBBEL
LYON, LUCIUS
MANNING, RANDOLPH
McCLELLAND, ROBERT
McDONELL, JOHN
MILLER, LEWIS T.
MOORE, WILLIAM
MORRIS, BENJ. B.
MUNDY, E.
NEWBERRY, SENECA
NEWTON, JAMES

MEMBERS OF CONVENTION.

NOBLE, NATHANIEL
NORVELL, JOHN
ODELL, JAMES
OTIS, ASA H.
PATRICK, WILLIAM
PATTERSON, JOSEPH H.
PORTER, HENRY
PORTER, SOLOMON
PURDY, ROBERT
RAYNALE, EBENEZER
REXFORD, ROSWELL B.
SHATTUCK, GILBERT
SHELLHOUSE, MARTIN G.
STEVENS, AMOS
STUBBS, M. P.
SUTPHEN, J. V. D.
TALLMAN, THEOPHILUS
TAYLOR, JOSHUA B.
TEN EYCK, J.
TIFFANY, ALEXANDER R.
TUCKER, JACOB
VAN EVERY, PETER
VOORHEIS, ISAAC J.
WADHAMS, RALPH
WELCH, WILLIAM H.
WELLS, HEZEKIAH G.
WHITE, ALPHEUS
WHITE, DAVID
WHITE, ORRIN
WHITE, SAMUEL

WILLIAMS, JOHN R.
WILKINS, ROSS
WILLARD, TITUS B.
WOODBRIDGE, WILLIAM

NAMES OF DELEGATES IN THE CONSTITUTIONAL CONVENTION OF 1850.

ADAMS, P. R.
ADAMS, WALES
ALVORD, H. J.
ANDERSON, R. H.
ARZENO, A. M.
AXFORD, W.
BACKUS, H. T.
BAGG, J. H.
BARNARD, ELI
BARTOW, H.
BARTOW, JOHN
BEARDSLEY, C. E.
BEESON, JACOB
BRITAIN, CALVIN
BROWN, ALVARADO
BROWN, AMMON
BROWN, ASAHEL
BURNS, J. D.
BUSH, C. P.
BUTTERFIELD, J. L.
CARR, W. S.
CHANDLER, C.
CHAPEL, C. W.
CHOATE, EMERSON

CHURCH, THOS. B.
CLARK, J.
CLARK, SAMUEL
COMSTOCK, A. J.
CONNER, W. O.
COOK, JOHN P.
CORNELL, J. G.
CRARY, ISAAC E.
CROUSE, ROBERT
DANFORTH, E. B.
DANIELS, EBENEZER
DESNOYERS, PETER
DIMOND, R. B.
EASTMAN, TIMOTHY
EATON, E. C.
EDMUNDS, J. M.
FRALICK, HENRY
GALE, ELBRIDGE G.
GARDINER, E. P.
GIBSON, JOHN
GOODWIN, DANIEL
GRAHAM, J.
GREEN, NELSON
HANSCOM, A. H.
HART, N. H.
HARVEY, G. C.
HASCALL, VOLNEY
HATHAWAY, H.
HIXON, DANIEL
KINGSLEY, JAMES

MEMBERS OF CONVENTION. 73

KINNE, DANIEL
LEACH, DEWITT C.
LEE, DANIEL S.
LOVELL, CYRUS
MARVIN, H. B.
MASON, LORENZO M.
McCLELLAND, ROBERT
McLEOD, WM. N.
MOORE, E. S.
MORRISON, W. V.
MOSHER, JOHN
MOWRY, Z. M.
NEWBERRY, SENECA
O'BRIEN, MORGAN
ORR, J. W. T.
PIERCE, J. D.
PIERCE, NATHAN
PREVOST, J. J.
RAYNALE, E.
REDFIELD, GEO.
ROBERTS, E. J.
ROBINSON, E. S.
ROBERTSON, A. S.
ROBINSON, RIX
ROBINSON, M.
SKINNER, E. M.
STOREY, WILBUR F.
STURGIS, D.
SOULE, MILO
SULLIVAN, JAMES

SUTHERLAND, J. G.
TIFFANY, A. R.
TOWN, OKA
VAN VALKENBURGH, J.
WAIT, W. B.
WALKER, D. C.
WARDEN, ROBERT
WEBSTER, JAMES
WELLS, H. G.
WHITE, J. R.
WHIPPLE, C. W.
WHITTEMORE, G. O.
WILLIAMS, JOSEPH R.
WILLARD, ISAAC, W.
WITHERELL, B. F. H.
WOODMAN, ELIAS

Charles M Croswell
President of the Convention
Adrian Mich

Thos H Glenn
Secretary Convention
Niles Mich

C. H. McCollum
1st Asst Sec'y
Pontiac Oakland
Co Mich
Yours truly, EVO [illegible]

Levi Aldrich
Edwardsburgh
Cass Co Mich

Wm W Andrus
Utica
Macomb co
Michigan

Lorenzo P Alexander
Buchanan
Berrien Co
Mich

A. Barber
Coldwater
Branch Co.
Mich

P. Bills
Tecumseh
Mich.

James Birney

Bay City

Mich

Asahel Brown

Algansee

Branch Co

Mich

S. H. Blackman
Paw Paw
Mich

Milton Bradley
Richland
Kalamazoo Co
Mich.

G. T. Case
Stanton
Montcalm Co
Mich

I am truly Your Friend &c
DeWitt C Chapin
Alma
Gratiot Co. M.

Bela Chapman
Mackinac Co
Mich

Milton P. M. Butler
Grand Ledge
Eaton Co
Mich

Henry H. Coolidge
Niles
Michigan

Yours Truly
O. D. Conger
Port Huron
St Clair Co
Michigan

Wm Corbin
Petersburg
Monroe Co
Mich

Nathaniel I. Daniells
Wacousta

Peter Demoyer
Detroit
Mich.

Delamore Duncan
Prairie Ronde
Kalamazoo Co.
Mich.

Charles Duncombe
Keeler
Van Buren Co
Mich

Adam Elliott Ell
Hickory Corners
Barry Co

D.B.W. Castle
Salt River
Isabella Co Mich

For the right
Sincerely Yours

Wm Smythe Farmer

Truly Yours
George W. German
North Plain
Boone Co

"Marsh Giddings
Kalamazoo

Edward P. Harr
Rochester
Oakland Co
Mich

Ezra Hagen
Memphis
St. Clair Co,
Mich,

E. F. Henderson
Marshall
Miet.

Daniel Hixson
Washtenaw Co.

C. D. Holmes
Albion
Mich

Henry H. Holt
Muskegon
Mich.

Sumner Howard
Flint Mich

Levi T Hull
Constantine
Mich

R. W. Hamlin Jr
Vassar
Tuscola Co
Mich

M. C. Kenny
Lapeer
Lapeer Co Mich

John M Lamb
Dryden M

B. W. Lanierer
  Hamby
Livingston Co.
  Mich

D.C. Leach
  Traverse City
    Mich.

Jno. W. Longyear
Lansing

H. R. Lovell
Flint
Mich

Cyrus G. Luce
Gilead
Branch Co

R. McClelland —
Detroit —
Mich. —

W M McConnell
Pontiac
Mich

J. C. McFernan Kinman
Houghton Co
Mich —

W. H. Miles
St Clair
St Clair Co

H. L. Miller
Saginaw City
Mich

E. V. Morton,
   Monroe,
      Mich.

Lyman Murray
   Alpine
      Kent Co, O

Dexter Mussey
Romeo
Macomb Co

Michigan
Charlott
Eaton Co

Thomas Ninde
Ypsilanti

Lyman D. Norris
Ypsilanti
Washtenaw

Kind regards of
Dan'l L Pratt
Hillsdale
Mich

Wm Purcell
Detroit
Mich

Eugene Pringle

Jackson. M.

Simeon P. Boal

Somerset Hillsdale Co

Mich

A Sawyer
Medina
Lenawee co
Mich

Horace J Sheldon
Sheffield
Lenawee
Mich

Truly Yours
Jonathan Shearer
Plymouth Wayne Co
Mich. —

T. G. Smith
Fenton
Genesee Co,
Mich

W. A. Smith
Redford
Wayne
Mich

M. P. Stockwell
Dover
Lenawee Co.
Mich

Wm S Stoughton

Sturgis
Mich

J. G. Sutherland
Saginaw City

L. C. Thompson
N. Adams
Hillsdale Co.
Mich.

Josiah Turner
Owosso
Mich

Comfort Tyler
Oporto
Saint Joseph County
Michigan

I am sir,
Yours Truly,
William S. Utley
Big Prairie
Ronagoleu,
Mich.

Julian Vankenburgh
White Lake
Oakland County

A H Walker
St Johns
Clinton Co
Mich

P. Dean Warner
Farmington
Oakland Co.

F. C. Watkins,
Norvell
Jackson Co.
Mich

M. C. Watkins
Grattan
Kent &

Wm. E. White
Wayland
Allegan Co
Mich

George Willard
Battle Creek,
Mich.

W. B. Williams
Allegan
Mich

Richard Winsor
Huron City
Mich

E B Winans

Hamburg

Livingston

Mich

S L Withey

Grand Rapids

Mich

S Stoddehouse
Dansville
Ingham Co
Mich

Sanford A. Yeomans
Ionia
Ionia Co.
Mich

Yours Truly,
William E Warner
Detroit

Charles K. Backus,
Correspondent Tribune & [Tribune?]
Detroit

Wm Blair Lord.
New York [City]
Official Reporter of Con"
Eng, NP, W, Mich

D. B. Purinton
Sergt-at-Arms of Convention
Cold Water Mich

B. Rice
Saginaw City
mich
Leonhardt Rich
Zingen am Rhein

George H Seymour
General M'f'g
Grand Rapids
Mich

Chauncey S Wright
Genr Mer
Fenton
Mich

Printed in Dunstable, United Kingdom